The Bones That Map Us

Poems

Maggie Rue Hess

BELLE POINT PRESS
Fort Smith, Arkansas

THE BONES THAT MAP US

Cover image: Getty Images via Canva Pro License
Author photo: Erin Morrison Photography

Edited by Casie Dodd
Design & typography by Belle Point Press

Belle Point Press, LLC
Fort Smith, Arkansas
bellepointpress.com
editor@bellepointpress.com

Find Belle Point Press
on Facebook, Substack,
and Instagram (@bellepointpress)

Printed in the United States of America

28 27 26 25 24 1 2 3 4 5

ISBN: 978-1-960215-14-7

CHAP10/BPP22

In memory of Karen L. Jasper

my wound has been my healing,
And I am made more beautiful by losses.
—Howard Moss

Contents

We know the ending but not the beginning, i

Our mom met our father

they divorced

* * *

the story of our father—

he

went

away

a stranger

and is

gone now

Runner at the Graveyard

My mother paid her respects to good health by walking through the town cemetery on Monday mornings. The one time I joined her on the circled asphalt path, she pointed to a granite marker: "I like the dark ones best. That's the kind I want." My mother healed people for a living; she knew their ligaments better than their names. She knew the reaper's handshake better than her wedding vows. How peaceful to be alive and know just how you want your death objectified; how comfortable you must be with loss. When life has taken from you repeatedly with no mercy for mortality, you learn to laugh about bones, how 206 of them will crumble; you begin to smile when you see the hearse as merely spacious transportation; you lace up a pair of sneakers and run among the headstones, plastic lilies, mausoleums, engravings, and statues littering our lost loves' last lands. I visited the graveyard when the clouds stole indigo from the evening sky, when the sky inhaled before the rain, and I jogged past a silent roll call until my lungs ached and my side stitched from breathing so desperately, and I could not have felt more alive.

I Do (Not Know)

My mother never told us what my stepfather said
when he proposed.

She followed him up a mountain, and
came back down with a secret she
promised to tell me on my own betrothal.

So this is how we pass on love:
it is a mystery we expect,
the success predetermined by the brevity,

women knowing only to believe
what they don't tell their daughters.

Better Jokes

In *Wonder Woman*,
the spy explains to the Amazonian
that marriage is a vow to love, honor,
cherish 'til death—she asks
if people keep it. "Not very often, no."
A familiar punchline.

. . .

The amputee jokes—all the time—
but especially about his remarriage.
This includes the fact that his new wife
already bought a grave site beside
her deceased prior husband, which the family
feels somewhat bad about

until after the jokes become taunts,
until the wife reveals her alcoholism,
until she dies in the middle of their divorce.
Then it seems fitting.
He told better jokes than vows, anyway.

If His Vows Were Honest

Oh my dear and constant strife,
I've been several different beasts
as long as you've known me—

Let's just grow old
disagreeing together.

I'd keep you hanging around
my neck, for the loveliest pendant
is a millstone.

Promise me, oh swear
if you must (*What the fuck?*)
to marry our resentment and apathy,
and I'll take the surname
Bitterness
to hate and to hold.

We know the ending but not the beginning, ii

Our mom tells the story of how she met our father—
to three daughters, each a separate time—

There are three stories,
and we don't know which is true, if any of them are.

* * *

Our mom tells the story of how she met our father—

He was taking classes

studying statistics
He was her patient
at physical therapy (one of her first)
because he had back problems
They met again in a laundromat

a romance began,
followed by a family.

our parents are gone now,
and with them, our origins.

* * *

Our mom tells the story of how she met our father—

He was
working a random job. At that point
in a warehouse.
He was
at her physical therapy job
because he had knee problems.
They met again in a bar.

a romance began,
followed by a family.

Both our parents are gone with the
shared history

* * *

Our mom tells the story of how she met our father—

they went to the same park and
one day his dog got off leash and ran away,
so she joined in with a few strangers
to find the dog (which they did).
the case may be, a romance began,
followed by a family.

Both our parents are gone now, and with them
a shared history   our origins.

Marriage Advice and Sauvignon Blanc

Sometimes you learn from others' misfortune;
sometimes you learn from others' experience.
Eventually, you will know the difference.
The night comes easily, like a three-year-long conversation,
but familiarity can't subvert what is magical:
a baseball field stunned by lightning bugs.
And then two glasses of white wine,
which gift you with fruited and easy tongues.
It's a night you didn't know you were waiting for,
just as you say the name you haven't felt
comfortable breathing so often until now.
Experience pours out two healthy cups
of sweetness, of rancor, of opposition,
and your mouth studies these, tasting
the bouquet of union.

Divorce Spoons

I don't know if we're facing our demons
or living with our omens:

The spoons we use for cereal,
for fruit cups, for sauces, for soups,
for mixing his coffee (cream, less sugar)
and mine (cream, more sugar)—
belonged to his former lover and her ex-husband.

The spoons we use
once loved their hands, the soft bridge
between need and sustenance
that marriage constructed, divorce removed.
When his former lover left her husband,
she kept the silverware. When he left
his lover, she left it behind.

And now they nestle in our drawers;
we heat them with our palms,
we slide them on our tongues.
We've grown comfortable with
a past that became a necessity.

Calling Dr. Freud

Isn't it strange to pick a lover
from the land of my father's exile?

You blind yourself trying
to undo your mother's mistakes.

How much more can we
be a Greek myth?

The riddle seals the relationship,
and the pleasure stages the tragedy.

We know the ending but not the beginning, iii

Our mom tells the story of how she met our father—
to three daughters, each a separate time—almost
twenty years after they divorced. He was taking classes
or working a random job. At that point
he was studying statistics or working in a warehouse.
He was her patient or someone else's
at her physical therapy job (one of her first)
because he had back problems or knee problems.
They met again in a laundromat or a bar.
Or they went to the same park and
one day his dog got off leash and ran away,
so she joined in with a few strangers
to find the dog (which they did).
Whatever the case may be, a romance began,
followed by a family. There are three stories,
and we don't know which is true, if any of them are.
Both our parents are gone now, and with them
a shared history; and with them, our origins.

* * *

Our mom tells the story of how she met our father—
                                        a separate time—almost
twenty years after they divorced

to find
What began
a family. There
is

a history with them, our origins.

Bleeding Hearts

Born of the arching stem,
born of the aching, stemming

from the break, daughter *dicentra*—
I will not pursue the obvious

metaphor, the perennial memory
of my mother and the old house,

the bushes crowding our front porch.
I will not grow my own suffering

for a poem. Every blossom
pinks its own becoming,

splits at a knowing touch.
Survival is a thirst and many arms.

The Bones That Map Us

Side by side
in the diner,
Gram and I
read menus;
my beloved
reads the bones
of our faces.
The two Maggies,
the family resemblance.

I used to look
like my mother.
She's become
the missing link
in a chain
of same-faced women:
Mom,
why did you
weary the bones
that map us?

Hers Was the Body: Wounded Healer

There are people who love my mother who did not see her
grotesque legs, swollen and aching. She would

dip them in the pool, kick at the edge with the grace
of an unconcerned lifeguard. Reduce her life

down to facts and they still wouldn't know
who she was: wounded healer, tired survivor.

She wore pink to her last wedding, but every color looked good
on her skin. Hers was the body she loved least,

whittled down until it was too small to save, too unruly to restore.
In the end she was so lonely. When she called, we said goodbye

but never I love you. I am so stubborn
                                        this regret raised itself in our silence.

Heavy My Blood

I remember learning about fish
in competitions being unzipped
at the stomach if they came in
just a little too heavy, learned
that fishermen would pour mercury
pellets down their throats to win
for weight. So heavy my blood
feels, afternoons in a starfish pose
on the bed, as if my limbs retracted,
useless fins above water. Think of me
breathing in a lake, catching silt in my gills,
unable to be a filter or even a worthy prize,
empty-bellied of mercury or seaweed or joy.

Hunger

So-
me-
times
I feel like
a spi-
ne with hips. A
wide
emp-
ti-
ness.

Hers Was the Body: Pain Management

my mother was an organ donor   I think   but when she died   I think   she didn't donate
that which had failed her most   her family   circumscribed the hospital bed   learned
machine sounds, machine numbers   the human goal was pain management   it's what they
tell you   when they can't save the patient   I like it though   it meant somebody was
trying   for her   when she tried for so many years   to heal the broken   to hide the shame
to keep the marriage   to raise the children   to run the business   in her final hour
it was all we could do   manage her pain   as if it hadn't been years   of erosion
if any body was deserving of rest   hers was   the body:
a temple   and   its sacrifice

Ghazal for a Pulse

I've known since I took swimming lessons at 8 how to check for a pulse,
because they teach CPR to everyone using the university pools.

Two fingers on a forearm—or neck—seeking the right artery;
a patient slowing of breath so you don't hear your own pulse.

When I hold my lover's hand, I press into his exposed wrist
to feel it, something to carry me close to his heart: his pulse.

Never love a rhythm more than you prepare for its absence.
The heart is a muscle that weakens despite all its pulls.

I knew in the transplant unit when my mother lived through machines
that cared intensively, but not enough, that it wasn't hers, the pulse

so strong, so constant, the things she'd forgotten to be. But still, I found
the heartbeat—something to carry me close to goodbye. Her pulse

pretended the syllables I already missed, *Maggie, daughter, I love,*
I love, until it slowed. When it stopped, the silence had a pulse.

At the adult beginner Spanish online night class

on the evening we learn how to
say words for family members,
when the teacher hasn't asked
anyone about their parents
and my turn is coming up—I just
know it—I mentally practice
how to tell the class
what I still have, because
I am always reaching for
the language to tell people
what I still have, and that's
when she calls on me:
Maggie, sus padres viven?
and even though I knew
she'd ask, I don't know how
she decided on that version,
not the usual *Do you have parents?*
that I'm used to interpreting,
so now all I can say is no
and mute myself. In the
ensuing discomfort I Google
huérfana so I know how to say
what I am, though when
you say orphan you don't picture

the 20-something adjusting her accent
over Zoom—you picture
some despondent, lonely child
who maybe speaks Spanish
or maybe doesn't
speak at all anymore or
something similarly pathetic,
but either way everyone responds
with their sad faces and sad voices,
so of course I can never be sad
when I talk about it—
it's okay, I'm okay, está bien –
when of course I don't mean that
and right now I'd rather say
yo tengo hermanas y un hermano
yo tengo mi abuela y abuelo
tuve una madre
I have, I have, I had.
I am
still learning
what
to say.

An Alcoholic's Daughter Edits the Dictionary

Haunted:

bitter adjective
1. Our parents die, and still they might try to kill us.
Somewhere my thirst is shaped like a coffin.
How many bottles wait to swallow me.

> An antonym for unnoticed, the way I bite my nails
> and paint over them weekly; for unloved,
> there is no approximation.

uncertain verb
1. Memory takes its first breath after its last birthday.
What kind of heart ruptures at random?
What kind of heart disappears its future rhythm?

> A synonym for echo, like stumbling footfalls
> and every time I hear "potassium."
> Who still pictures a banana when
> there are muscles that could stop.

The origin of the word: a laugh in an empty room
[count the syllables like an audience of one]

The Heart of Texas Goes Cold

It's a Texas chill, so our feet touch
below the covers, sole to toe.

We lament the winters we've lost
until a day returns them to us,
then we go silent. I take this for granted,

being cold and knowing how to find warmth
and, even more, having that from someone else.

If you left, would I ever stop
telling people about you? Where
would I put my feet?

Scared / Sacred

My mother had four husbands
and died in the middle
of her last divorce.

Hon, these are the only
blueprints I have:
you leave, one way or the other.

I've hardly seen
a successful marriage up close.
When Mom remarried
the second time, she had
three years. He was
only 30 when his Jeep
flipped in a country ditch.

Hon, all I know is
I could lose you,
one way or the other.

A headache, kidney stones,
chest pains, these
unforgivable mortalities.

Every day I love you,
I wed my fear.

I bless every year of you,
every scared, sacred
year of you.

Funny Like That

I

When they say “grief is funny like that,” turns out they really do mean
it’s funny, like laughing for 6 minutes uninterrupted at something your lover said
without thinking they were silly until you can’t breathe and your cheeks are rivers
because you have laughed into the tears you knew you were going to cry hours ago
but did not have a reason to. You cry every week. There is rarely a full reason to cry
except that someone you loved died some time ago and you have not forgotten it yet,
not your brain or your heart or your tear ducts, so that something goes wrong or
a snatch of song moves you or your lover tosses off a comment strikingly hilarious
and you do not even pretend to hold back what you spent two decades avoiding
with all your might and it seems like you are bursting at the seams in giggles
when you are really so sad so deep down and only you knew grief is funny like that.

II

When grief is out
it's some lover
thinking they were your rivers
you have laughed the tears you were going to cry
You cry every week. There is rarely a reason
someone you loved you have not forgotten
your heart goes wrong
a song moves you strikingly
and you do not hold back avoiding
all your bursting
when you are really so sad so funny like that.

III

grief is

some lover

they were rivers

you were going to cry

every week. There is a reason

someone loved you

your heart

a song

and you do not hold back

so sad so funny

Of Course All Dogs Go to Heaven

In my Heaven,
the angels are all dogs.

It's not a very mature
reading of the Bible,
but I have believed
so many wrong things already—
this one is harmless.

Looking for an Ear

My sister is looking for an ear.
She is looking through her daughter,
through her nephew.
She is looking for her partner,
looking for her mother, her father,
looking for her grandparents.
She is asking our older sister
and she is asking me
about the curve of the cartilage
and the length of the lobe
and the hint of heredity
that we all wonder about
when we see newborns or ourselves
growing the faces that may someday
lead us back to our families.
We see her newborn
and we see ourselves
and we see our family,
a body growing outward from a heart.
We are the ears and mysteries
that lineage makes as an unspoken promise.

Summer Ages

for Austin

We sit in cheap chairs in the yard, mulberries
unripe & fallen at our toes,
honeysuckle whispering sweetness
from the brush. The shade
is spring qua summer, the sun
preparing for its fullness.
You type distractedly,
nonprofit-excel-worksheet stressed.
Beside me I feel what Plato said I would
always search for.

We are 55 & deep in the season.

We are 83 years old, enjoying good weather.

We are 20 years old, just waiting for each other.

We are 34 & perfect.

I can spend hours not looking in your eyes
and my veins sing with you.

Acknowledgments

My gratitude belongs to the following journals, publications, and anthologies where these poems first appeared:
Tiny Spoon, "At the adult beginner Spanish online night class"
The Minnesota Review, "Heavy My Blood"
Feels Zine, "Looking for an Ear"
Scrawl Literary Magazine, "If His Vows Were Honest" (formerly "Proposal")
But There Was Fire in the Distance: Selections from Lexington Poetry Month 2021, "Hunger"
Red Branch Review, "Divorce Spoons"
Yearling, "Summer Ages"

Many thanks to the creative community of LexPoMo, who helped and hosted earlier versions of "The Bones That Map Us," "Marriage Advice and Sauvignon Blanc," "Scared / Sacred," and "Of Course All Dogs Go to Heaven," as well as the Tupelo Press 30/30 Project, which helped me produce drafts of "Funny Like That" and "Looking for an Ear."

Without the guidance of many friends and mentors, this collection would not have taken its first forms. Poetry (for me) is an act best realized in community.

To every friend who ever came to a reading or proudly introduced me as "a poet" & to every fellow poet who welcomed me: thank you.

To my teachers, David Swerdlow and Rebecca Gayle Howell, who treated each draft—and me as a writer, each step of the way—with earnestness and care.

To my workshop friends: Amber, Andrew, Ashley, Catie, Casey, Ace—without y'all most of these poems would not exist, or would not exist with as much precision.

To Caitlin, who has cheered me on since our Writers Guild days and read early versions of this chapbook with the total trust that it could be in the world someday.

To Grandma Peggy and Joel, who fed my love of reading and writing, and fed my dogs the best treats in town, you are my home away from home; Gram, I hope I wear your name well.

To Corey, Kylee, Serena, Michael, and Abby: I would not be me without you all. Thank you for keeping me close.

To Mom, who gifted me (among many other things) a copy of Mary Oliver's *New and Selected Poems, Volume 1,* as a souvenir from her trip to Alaska because, even though she didn't understand much poetry, she understood how much I loved it. That book and her love have directed my life in endless ways.

One night, some time after we were married, I cried on the couch about how I wished Mom were at the wedding to see that—after the years of warnings, spoken and unspoken—I'd done a good job: I'd found you. Austin, loving you is my good job, my best work, better than any poem. Thank you for reading my poems and loving me back and letting me hold your wrist every time I need something steady at my fingertips.

Maggie Rue Hess is a PhD student living in Knoxville, Tennessee, with her partner and their two crusty white dogs. Her work has appeared in *Rattle*, *Minnesota Review*, *Connecticut River Review*, and other publications; *The Bones That Map Us* is her debut chapbook. She serves as a poetry reader and Managing Editor for Online Content for *Grist: A Journal of the Literary Arts*. Maggie gets her stubbornness from both sides of her family and shares baked goods to show love; she has a surprising competitive side and her mom's crooked front teeth.

BELLE
POINT
PRESS